Blacksmit

Easy

Comprehensive Forging for Beginners Guide on How to Master the Art of Bladesmithing, Knife Making and Knife Engineering To Ultimately Make Cool, Out Of This World Blacksmithing Projects

Charles Prince

Introduction

Do you know where the knife originated? Did you also know that more than 2,000 years ago, there was a stone-age era where hominids shaped stones into tools used for cutting and digging?

While you may not be in touch with the past culture on knife making, the knife is one of a few ancient tools not replaced by other technologically advanced gadgets, which has been the case with most other tools replaced by technologically advanced models.

The knife has retained its usefulness as a simple blade used to carry out many tasks. This ancient, basic tool still has uses in kitchens and various other working spaces. You can carry it with you wherever you go, and it could save you from an unpleasant situation, especially if you love outdoor adventures.

Would you like to learn how to make a knife? Do knives fascinate you, and you would like to go a step further and make different types of knives? If so, you're reading the right book.

This guidebook will discuss the blacksmithing tools, strategies, and ideas you need as a beginner to create knives, including how to set up your workshop space and fashion different knife designs.

This comprehensive guide will do more than teach you how to make knives; it will also inspire you to create many other top-notch blacksmithing projects. After mastering the skills you will learn from this eBook, you may eventually discover that you want to turn your hobby into a money-making project.

Let's begin so you can discover more about knife making and become a master blacksmith.

PS: I'd like your feedback. If you are happy with this book, please leave a review on Amazon.

Please leave a review for this book on Amazon by visiting the page below:

https://amzn.to/2VMR5qr

Table of Content

Introduction _____ 2

Chapter 1: A Brief History Of Blacksmithing 6

Chapter 2: Planning Your Blacksmithing Workspace_____13

Chapter 3: Starter Tools For A New Blacksmith_____16

Chapter 4: Safety Rules Every Blacksmith Should Follow _____61

Chapter 5: Beginners Guide To Forging A Basic Knife_____71

   Forging A Six-Inch Survival Knife _____ 71

Chapter 6: The Best Projects For A Beginner Blacksmith_____ **83**

   Simple J Hook_____ 83

   Punch_____ 84

   Fire Poker _____ 85

Bottle Opener _____ 86

Decorative Heart _____ 87

Leaf Key Chain _____ 88

Rounding Hammer _____ 89

Dinner Bell _____ 91

Tongs _____ 92

Loggerhead _____ 94

Loop Opener _____ 95

Herb Chopper _____ 96

Egg Spoon and Ladle _____ 97

Colonial Spatula _____ 99

Meat Skewer _____ 102

Heart Decorative Bowl _____ 103

Drawer Pulls _____ 104

Conclusion _____ **105**

Chapter 1: A Brief History Of Blacksmithing

In the stone-age period, man used stone tools to complete various tasks such as digging and cutting.

Hand-ax stone tool in early Stone Age Europe

Early man created stone tools such as the hand-ax using a hammer-stone to strike or chip off flakes from rounded pebbles or large flakes. Before the metalworking age, that was a universal technology in many parts of the world, including Europe, North America, and India.

Different types of Hammer-stones

Shaping a stone into a cutting tool required great skill and extra caution because fashioning them could also easily destroy these tools. The primary disadvantage with stone tools is that they would not last long and needed frequent shaping and carving to work correctly.

Around 1200 BC, man discovered the art of smelting bronze to make tools. This technology further evolved when man innovated smelting pots that could withstand temperatures high enough to forge iron into tools.

An antique lead melting pot

The smelting process involves retrieving metal from its ore by heating it above the melting point in the presence of an oxidizing agent like air. This discovery, and the easy availability of iron ore, transformed how humans made usable tools across different cultures in many parts of the world.

He (man) then formed new tools, including metal axes used for clearing land for agricultural use and swords used as weapons in warfare.

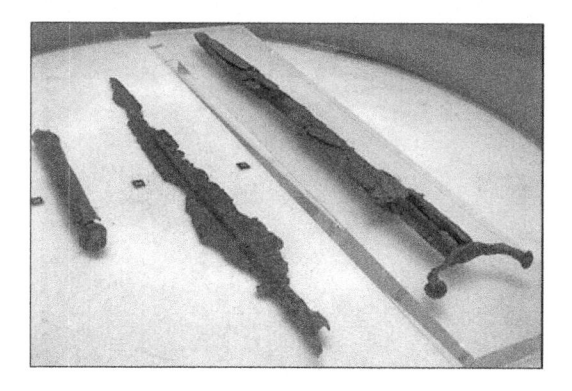

7th century BC Iron Swords from Italy

Blacksmithing continued evolving differently in various parts of the world. The anvil, the main tool used in blacksmithing, is a good example of how this trade has evolved. An anvil is a metalworking tool made from large blocks of metal with top surfaces that are flat on which another object gets struck, formed, and shaped.

Anvil

London pattern anvil

The first anvils were from primitive objects, mainly stone, usually a slab of rock. The anvil then graduated to a metal one, made from bronze, followed by wrought iron, and, lastly, steel. Steel is the most preferred metal used today for making anvils. Over the centuries, the shape of the anvil has evolved from just a simple slab to become the anvil known today as the 'London Pattern' that became popular in the 1800s.

While its size and length have changed with time in different parts of the world, the anvil's standard design consists of a horn, a face, a step, a pritchel hole, and a hardy hole.

The forge has also improved significantly over the centuries. The early forge was simply a pit of fire fueled by charcoal and motivated to burn with air from a pair of bellows made from leather and wood used to blow air into the fire to increase the temperature suitable enough for melting iron.

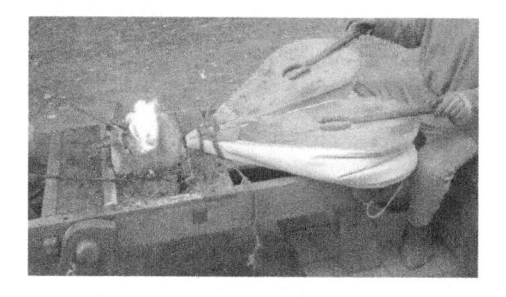

blacksmiths working old fashioned bellows

With time, this type of forge became raised a little higher off the ground. Coal eventually became the most common form of fuel used in the forges connected to blast pipes.

Today, the situation is slightly different as blacksmiths use propane gas and acetylene gas in their forges. An electrical forge is one of the latest innovations:

propane forge

mini electric forge

Historically, blacksmiths used iron wrought, a pure form of iron with very little added carbon. Today, however, it is difficult to find pure wrought iron. Therefore, blacksmiths use a type of iron called mild steel. As a result, the term 'iron' gets used for the mild steel that has replaced the pure wrought iron.

As a blacksmithing beginner, it's fundamental to understand that because the scarcity of wrought iron means you can use various types of steel for blacksmithing, including carbon steel, alloy steel, and tool steel, to name a few.

Having looked at a brief overview of how blacksmithing has evolved, let's discuss how to set up your blacksmithing workshop space:

Chapter 2: Planning Your Blacksmithing Workspace

Now that you have decided to be a blacksmith, how much workshop space do you need, and how much will it cost to set it up?

You should answer these questions carefully so that your blacksmithing workspace is neither too big nor too small. Your budget is the most determinant factor in the type and size of the workspace you create.

For starters, a space that is no more than 100 square feet is the most ideal for a blacksmith beginner. Even if you can afford to have a much larger workspace, stick to the recommended square feet. Adhering to this recommendation allows you to nurture your skill much better and become a more successful blacksmith. The small workspace provides a learning curve where you will be more effective and efficient.

Your tools placement system highly determines how quickly you work and how fast you learn your skill. A large workspace will entrap you to scatter your tools all over the workshop, decreasing your capacity to work swiftly, effectively, and efficiently.

Sooner or later, as you continue learning your new craft, you will discover that there's very little time to work on your steel once it leaves the forge. Picking your tongs, hammer, and getting to the anvil within the shortest time possible is extremely important.

As a beginner, have your anvil two paces away from your forge. Place your tools close and according to the order in which you will need to use them. For instance, place your tongs adjacent to the forge so that it will be easily accessible when you're about to remove a piece of hot steel out of the forge.

Furthermore, for a quick grab, place your hammer on or beside your anvil. By setting up your tools correctly, you'll spend less time at the forge, thus producing high-quality work more efficiently.

Beginners to this trade should avoid tools fashioned for more experienced blacksmiths. Such tools will only multiply your mistakes, which in most cases, are inevitable. For example, skilled blacksmiths know and understand how to use a high-end hydraulic press that practically replaces muscle function and improves work efficiency. For a beginner that attempts to use such equipment without the required experience, it hampers skill development. Making steel without a power press or hammer provides the learner with a much greater comprehension of the steel forging process.

A new blacksmith will learn more by understanding how and why failures occur when working on a metal piece. Being given all the answers without experiencing any failures will not equip you with the knowledge you need to become a successful blacksmith. Working from a smaller space with essential tools instead of high-end equipment will force you to be creative, improving your skills.

Now that we're talking about tools:

Chapter 3: Starter Tools For A New Blacksmith

You don't have to get all the tools and materials before you set up your blacksmithing workspace. All you need are essential tools, which include the following:

#: *The Anvil*

Is it necessary to work on an anvil as a blacksmith? Can't I hammer at my steel from your wooden workbench? As a beginner blacksmith, you might ask such questions.

The truth is that you will need a stable surface to work from when hammering your steel. You can work a stable iron or steel workbench. However, for most blacksmiths, an anvil is a necessary and highly recommended tool that helps produce excellent results. It's the main tool used in the blacksmithing trade.

The anvil is a block of steel or iron with a hard, flat, and smooth surface. This surface is where you shall beat metal pieces and mold them into the desired shape. Anvils can be very expensive; therefore, beginners should opt for a used, cheaper one. However, the most crucial objective is to get a good-quality anvil as you start your blacksmithing journey.

You can purchase used and new anvils from websites like eBay, Amazon, or Craigslist. By design, anvils last for a very long time, and many blacksmiths may use just one for a lifetime. If you can afford it, a new one is always a much better deal than a second-hand one, unless you desperately want a more traditional look.

The creators of the fascinating object called the anvil that's been in use for hundreds of years created it with deliberate functions. The anvil has different parts, with each serving a specific purpose, as you can see below:

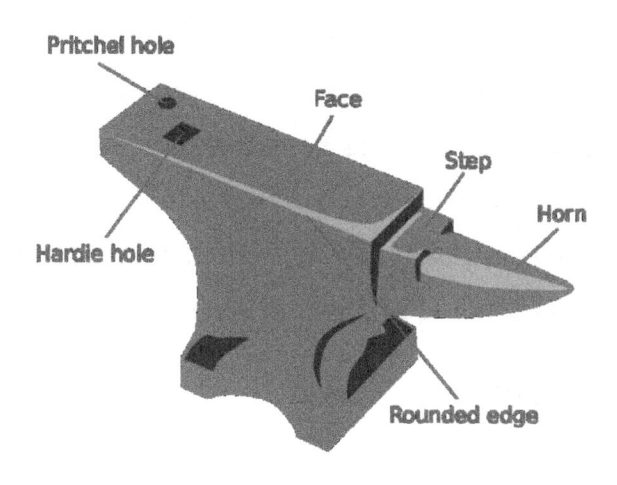

Part of an anvil

1: Face

The face is the largest part of the anvil. It's the elongated, flat section at the top, which is the platform used to place pounding-ready, hot metal. By design, the face can withstand the heavy pounding common with blacksmithing.

2: Step

The step is the area just below the face next to the horn. The edge of the step helps with cutting a piece of metal while hammering it. This part is prone to damage when used too frequently, which is why the tools used for cutting would be the most suitable.

3: Horn

The horn is the corn-shaped part of the anvil protruding on one side. It helps shape metal into curved or rounded shapes, something done by placing your hot working metal on this part, then hammering it into the desired shape. This part sometimes has a lesser strength than the face because its primary use is shaping and hammering.

4: Pritchel Hole

There are two holes on the anvil; the smaller one is the one called the pritchel hole. The purpose of this hole is to punch holes into hot metal pieces, something done by placing a chisel or any other suitable tool in the hole, with the hole punched by hammering the metal from the top.

5: Hardy Hole

This hole is bigger and rectangular, and its main use is holding various tools such as chisels and swages—Swages help shape metal. This hardy hole also directly aids in bending or punching holes.

What to look for in an Anvil

Anvils have different features depending on the manufacturer or brand. Thus, it's important to know what to look for in an anvil, which includes:

1: Weight and Size

As a beginner blacksmith, you need to ask yourself how you will be using your anvil—what purpose do you have for it?

Do you intend to forge knives and blade products? Are you planning to graduate from blade projects to larger ones sometime in the future? Such considerations will determine the weight and size of the anvil you should get.

The most appropriate anvil for beginners is small and lighter because it takes up less space in your workshop.

2: Material

Anvils manufacturers use different materials like steel or cast iron. Steel is usually preferred because iron can be brittle.

Furthermore, iron anvils have quite a lot of rebound when hit with a hammer. Steel has less rebound when struck by a hammer. Most anvils are steel slabs, meaning you have various steel anvils to choose from when purchasing one.

You can also find exotic anvils made from stone or bronze, but they're not easy to come by—or pocket-friendly for that matter.

New blacksmiths need simpler anvils, not exotic ones or those made from stone or bronze. As you mature in the trade, you may then try out the more complicated designs.

3: Cost

Cost is a crucial factor when considering which anvil to buy. Most anvils are not as expensive as you would think, though there are some costly ones.

The cost of an anvil can also depend on the material used to make it. Smaller anvils can cost between $3 and $4 per pound. Larger ones can cost $8 or more per pound.

A 50-pound anvil would cost you between $100 and $150, and a larger 100-pound anvil could cost you around $500 or more. Anvils costing $200 and $300 are the most ideal for new blacksmiths.

Different types of Anvils

Beginner blacksmiths need to know and understand different types of anvils. Discussed below are a few examples of anvils you can find in the marketplace:

1: Cast Iron Anvils

120 Pound Cast-Iron anvil

A cast-iron anvil is a more traditional tool still used and respected by skilled blacksmiths. They are much cheaper than most anvils, and in the current marketplace, they're not as many as steel anvils.

As the name suggests, manufacturers create cast iron anvils from an alloy with a considerable amount of carbon—compared to regular iron.

One disadvantage of the cast-iron anvil is that it can be brittle than most other types of anvils because they easily chip under consistent hammering. While the iron-cast anvil is much cheaper and can still get the job done, many blacksmiths now consider it low quality than the latest versions of anvils.

2: Farrier Anvils

Farrier anvil

Like the cast-iron, the farrier is another traditional anvil mostly found in farms where there are horses because farm owners use it to curve metal for a horseshoe.

The farrier anvil looks just like the normal anvil but has a slightly different shape. The mass is distributed differently from the usual anvil. It has a larger horn and a much smaller face because these anvil parts help make the horseshoes.

Although made from a much harder iron, the farrier is lightweight, made so because the blacksmiths that made horseshoes had to move with their anvils from one farm to another as they were required to either forge or adjust horseshoes.

3: Forging Anvils

A typical forging anvil

The forging anvil has become the most popular anvil among modern blacksmiths. Unlike the farrier and cast-iron anvils with more specialized uses, forging anvils can handle much heavier blacksmith projects.

The face of this type of anvil is large compared to the cast-iron and farrier anvils, providing more space to hammer at your working metal. It also has a considerably large horn.

Apart from the first two anvils, forging anvils are steel-fashioned, meaning they can withstand hammer blows and don't chip easily. That's why they are suitable for blacksmiths who are new to the trade because the anvil rebounds less when hit by a hammer. With much fewer rebounds, you will be able to hammer more strokes without your arm, wrist, and hand getting tired very fast.

Forging anvils are much heavier than cast-iron or farrier anvils tha have a weight of between 150 and 200 pounds.

Recommended anvil for beginners

You might go for the cast iron because it is a lot cheaper than other anvils. However, forging anvils are the most recommended for blacksmith beginners because their design means they can handle massive amounts of forces and pressure from a pounding hammer.

If you intend to be in this trade for a very long time, then the forging anvil is more durable than the cast iron anvil. The cast iron anvil deteriorates with time as it slowly chips away after frequent hammer hits.

One of the highly recommended anvils for beginners is the Cliff Carroll 35 pound anvil. This anvil is ideal for beginners because it is light, cheap, simple, and easy to work with and handle.

Weighing at 35 pounds, this is a much cheaper anvil in the market today. It costs only $200, making it cheap compared to what is available in the market. You can get one from one of the highly recommended blacksmith shops called Centaur Forge in North America.

Cliff-Carroll-35-lb-Anvil

#: Hammers

We have a wide variety of blacksmith hammers that all serve different purposes. There are many factors to consider when choosing a hammer, especially as a beginner.

For instance, you should consider your skill level and the purpose for which you will use your hammer, whether it is making blades or general blacksmithing.

Choosing the correct hammer, especially for a beginner, is usually an uphill task, more so because selecting the wrong style, type, or weight can frustrate your skill progression and the outcome of your work.

blacksmith hammer

Factors to consider when choosing a hammer

Here're some of the essential things you should consider when choosing a blacksmithing hammer:

1: Type and style of hammer

Blacksmithing hammers come in different types and styles, but as a general rule, most hammers have two ends that can either be of the same or different shape.

Hammers with different styles, heads, and patterns

We usually call these ends the face of the hammer. Hammers with different patterned faces, either flat or curved, directly affect the final metal piece's shape. The varieties of hammers available for blacksmiths differ based on their core designs and function. There are many types of hammers, including ball peen, sled hammer, cross peen, etc.

Hammers can have similar designs but still have not-easily-noticeable differences. These tiny differences often relate to their overall style, which indicates the country of origin. For example, we have Swedish styles like the Swedish cross peen hammer, or the German styles called the German-Style Cross Pein hammer. Some of the styles include Swedish, Japanese, French, and New England patterns.

Although they look similar, the tiny differences in hammer shape and form can alter its function altogether.

Different styles of Swedish cross peen blacksmith hammers

2: Weight and Usability

A hammer's ease of use is a significant factor that a beginner blacksmith should consider when deciding what hammer to buy. A hammer's weight can either make it easy to use or not, depending on your skills or strength.

A lighter hammer is ideal and recommended for new blacksmiths because it can help you hone your hammering skills without the tool's weight limitations. In general, choosing a hammer for a particular purpose is more important than its weight.

3: New versus Used hammers

The style and material used to make a hammer determine its cost. High-quality, durable hammers are expensive than low-quality ones. As a beginner, you may opt to purchase used hammers that, besides being affordable, will also last.

4: Wooden, plastic, and fiber-glass hammer handles

Although plastic and fiber-glass handles are very comfortable to work with, wooden handles are the best option when working on hot metal pieces. Because of its proximity to the heat, the fiber-glass and plastic handles will deform over time.

The best blacksmith hammers for beginners

Now that you know and understand the different factors to consider when choosing a hammer, which one is most suitable for a beginner?

Below are two examples of hammers that blacksmith beginners can start with:

1: Black Smith Ball Peen (Pein) Hammer

Black Smith Ball Peen

The ball-peen hammer—also called the peening hammer—has two different faces: one rounded, known as the peen, and a flat one. It resembles a household hammer because one of its faces is flat.

Peening is the process by which the metal worked on receives its shape and form because of repeated hammer blows. The head, which is a strong metal, is made from high-carbon steel, and the material that makes the handle is wooden.

This particular hammer is excellent for working on knives and swords because it easily smoothes out dents using the hammer's flat side. It has a low weight ranging between 1 to 3 pounds.

2: Blacksmith Cross Peen (Pein) Hammer

Blacksmith Cross Peen

The cross peen hammer is a popular choice for blacksmiths because it serves different purposes. One end of the hammerhead has a flat face, and the other is a narrow wedge-like face called the cross peen.

Because it's an all-purpose hammer, this hammer is an excellent choice for beginners. The parallel cross peen allows you to hammer small objects without accidentally hurting your fingers.

They come in different styles, such as French, German, and Swedish, giving you various styles from which to choose. They are available in weights ranging between 2 and 3 pounds, which is ideal for a beginner.

#: A Forge

The forge is where metal gets heated at very high temperatures, making it easier to bend and shape.

As a beginner, you can either make a forge or buy one. Forges come in different sizes and shapes. There are two main types of forges, including the non-solid fuel forge and the solid fuel forge. With two conventional fuels used in the forge, propane and coal, you ought to decide what type of fuel you want to use.

Consider buying a forge you can easily control. The forge is the most expensive tool in blacksmithing and can range between $200 and $500.

Hell's Forge Portable Propane Forge Single Burner Knife and Tool Making Farrier Forge

Hell's forge is an excellent forge you can buy for smaller projects such as forging knives.

#: *Tongs*

Tongs help hold your work firmly as you remove it from the forge and work on it on the anvil. It enables you to hold your metal red hot metal piece in place as you hammer at it.

Tongs allow you to manipulate and move your work-piece with ease, efficiency, and accuracy while keeping your fingers safe from the hammer. Since tongs come in different styles and types, how do you choose the one suitable for your needs?

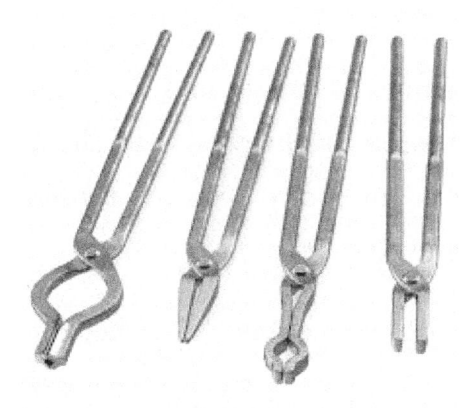

blacksmith tongs

As is the case with hammers, when buying a pair of tongs, you ought to consider various factors, including:

1: The tongs' anatomy

As a beginner, you need to understand the different aspects of tongs before purchasing any.

We call the tongs' handles reins and use them to open and close your pair of tongs. Opening and closing the tongs is possible because of the joint located where the reins meet. The joint has a rivet and a hinge plate to hold the two reins together.

We call the part ahead of the joint the jaws. The jaws are the ones that grasp and grip the hot metal-pieces. The tongs' jaws can have different shapes for different functions.

2: Tongs' length

Tongs come in different lengths and range between 15 and 40 inches. Longer tongs are heavier than shorter ones. Unlike shorter ones, long tongs also keep you further away from the forge's flames and heat.

The tongs' length can either be a benefit or hindrance. Therefore, you need to identify the most suitable one depending on your expertise, skill, and type of project on which you will be working.

A tong of between 18 and 20 inches, such as the V-bit bolt tongs, wolf jaw tongs, and the Z-jaw tongs, will be perfect for beginners.

3: Weight and type of tongs

It's difficult to recommend the best weight for your tongs because people are different. Some prefer working with lighter tongs, while others do very well with heavier tongs.

Most beginners find it easier to start with a light tong as they get used to the physical exertion and movements while working on a blacksmithing job.

Types of blacksmithing tongs ideal for a beginner

Below are two examples of tongs ideal for a beginner blacksmith:

1: V-Bolt tongs

V-Bolt tongs

V-bit tongs have a circular shape close to the joint when the tongs are in a closed position. The ends of the bits are parallel to the rest of the tong while in the closed position. Each bit has v-shaped sides.

This type of tongs can handle various functions, but its most common use is knife-making. The v-bits provide a strong grip on the knife's blade while a blacksmith shapes it.

2: Wolf jaw tongs

Wolf jaw tongs

Wolf jaw tongs are great for beginners because of their multi-purpose functions. They are lightweight and yet tough enough to withstand forging force and pressure. Its wavy tooth-like shape provides a firm grip that can handle different shapes and sizes of metal pieces.

#: *Clamp or Vice*

A vice or clamp is a tool that helps you achieve great results with your metalwork. It works best when it has a fastener, allowing the metal to withstand repeated hammer hits. They are readily available in the market and are affordable.

Forged C Clamp

#: Steel

Selecting the right steel to work with can be daunting because we have varieties of steel of different alloys and grades, making it challenging to decide on the correct one. That is why, as a beginner, you need to familiarize yourself with the categories of metals used in blacksmithing so that you can narrow down your selection process.

Here's a breakdown of some of the most common types of steel you will encounter in the market, including the advantages and disadvantages of each type:

1: Carbon Steels

Carbon steel is the most common steel blacksmiths use to make their products. This type of steel does not contain more than 2% alloy elements. It does not have any minimum specified amount of elements, including nickel, chromium, titanium, or any other variety of elements that manufacturers can add to achieve steel with alloy characteristics.

More categorically, carbon steel contains a maximum copper content of 0.60%, a maximum silicon content of 0.60%, and a maximum manganese content of 1.65%.

Carbon-steel

A: Low to mild carbon steels

This group of carbon steels has 0.30% carbon and is the largest of the three. It can create a diversity of structures and shapes and is handy for making such items as hooks and railings. They come in the form of flat support beams or metal sheets.

Mild carbon steel

B: Medium carbon steels

This type of steel contains 0.31% to 0.60% carbon. The higher carbon makes this steel stronger than lower carbon steel. However, that also makes shaping it difficult. This metal is ideal for making items such as hammers, gears, bolts, and nuts.

Medium carbon steel

C: High carbon steel

These types have over 0.61% carbon content. Because of the comparatively high carbon in this type of steel, it is difficult to shape and brittle. It is also very tough because of the high carbon content, making it the most suitable metal for making swords, nails, knives, and metal-cutting tools.

High carbon steel

Forging temperature for carbon steels

The level of temperature applied to steel depends on its carbon content. The higher the carbon content, the less temperature it needs. The color of steel changes depending on the amount of heat applied to it. Carbon steel requires temperatures of between 2200 degrees Fahrenheit to 2300 degrees Fahrenheit to forge.

As a blacksmith, you can know the temperature at which you are forging the metal by observing the steel change color as you heat it. However, that is only possible if you are in a shaded workspace, which makes this method **NOT** 100% authentic but still a good indicator of the temperature you are forging your metal piece.

Advantages and disadvantages of Carbon Steel

Carbon steel has a wide array of applications and is readily available in the market. Recycled carbon steel is also available in the market, but you have to be careful because its components are not easy to determine.

Manufacturers can add lead and zinc to recycled steel, which can be dangerous because it releases harmful fumes while forging. Be extra cautious when buying recycled steel because, in most cases, it is difficult to derive its components with certainty.

Here're it's advantage and disadvantages:

Advantages

- You can fashion it into a variety of shapes
- Affordable
- It can make all kinds of items, including tools and blades
- Its properties are alterable to varying degrees

Disadvantages

- Can rust and corrode easily depending on the type of steels

- Low carbon steel requires high temperatures for forging

- Hardened carbon steel can be extremely brittle and hence can break easily

- Can be tough to shape depending on the carbon content

#: *Alloy steels*

Although steel is an alloyed metal, alloy steel is a distinct type of steel in the sense that it has components added on purpose to change its properties.

Some of these properties include resistance, formability, ductility, and harden-ability. The materials used to prepare alloy steel include vanadium, tungsten, nickel, manganese, and chromium.

Alloy Steels Composition

Alloy steels can be high alloy or low alloy steel. High alloy steel has more than 10% of alloying components other than iron or carbon. On the other hand, Low alloy has less than 0.2% carbon content, with its alloying elements made up of less than 10% of its composition.

Alloy steel is easy to alter into the desired shape and is inexpensive as well. Chromium increases toughness, hardness, and wear resistance, manganese hardens the steel's surface, provides shock and stain resistance, and nickel offers resistance to oxidation and corrosion and increases the steel's toughness and strength.

Tungsten hardens the steel, improves its grain structure, and makes it resistant to heat. Vanadium provides resistance to corrosion and shock and increases the steel's strength and toughness.

Advantages and disadvantages of alloy steel

Alloy steel has many more uses than carbon steel because it is generally stronger, harder, has extra ductile properties, and higher corrosion resistance, which is why the aerospace and construction industries use it so much. Its magnetic characteristic makes it an excellent choice for electronic items.

Advantages

- It's easy to process
- It has magnetic properties
- Its properties, including various alloying elements, are improvable
- Compared to carbon steel, it has increased hardness, toughness, formability, ductility, and resistance to corrosion when

Disadvantages

- It is more expensive than carbon steel
- It is brittle at high-stress levels
- It needs heat treatment
- May require special handling

#: *Stainless Steel*

Stainless is a type of metal resistant to corrosion discovered in the early 20th century. Stainless steel has 10% chromium, making it high alloy steel. Chromium is the alloying element in stainless steel that produces chromium oxide when it reacts with atmospheric gases.

The chromium oxide acts as a form of self-repair that builds on the steel's surface, preventing any stain or rust. This reaction gives it a lustrous appearance as opposed to the dull look of regular carbon steel. Because of its attractive finish, stainless steel is a popular choice for making decorative products.

Stainless steel Composition

There are four stainless steel groups: ferritic stainless steel, austenitic stainless steel, martensitic stainless steel, and duplex stainless steel.

1: Ferritic Stainless Steel

It's magnetic with a high chromium content of 27%.

2: Austenitic stainless steel

It has high chromium content with 8% nickel in it. Its primary use is manufacturing equipment for the medical and food industry.

3: Martensitic stainless steel

It is magnetic with up to 1% molybdenum. The ductility property in this type of stainless steel makes it easy to create various shapes. It's primary use it to make blades and machine parts.

4: Duplex stainless steels

Duplex stainless steel is a mixture of austenitic stainless steel and ferritic stainless steel. This steel has a high molybdenum and chromium content, making it much tougher and stronger than austenitic and ferritic stainless steels.

This stainless steel's primary use is making food processing and chemical processing equipment mainly because it can tolerate severe environments.

Forging temperature for stainless steel

Stainless steel is compatible with various substances, making it an attractive material for chemical processes that require much higher temperatures. Depending on its grade, stainless steel is moldable in temperatures between 1700 degrees Fahrenheit and 2100 degrees Fahrenheit.

To improve its formability, manufacturers often add nickel and molybdenum to the stainless steel. The mechanical properties are enhance-able by forging, leading to a more robust and more resistant material.

Advantages and disadvantages of stainless steel

Although stainless steel has a thermal conductivity lower than carbon steel, it finds extensive use in manufacturing industrial and domestic appliances because of its high resistance to oxidation and corrosion.

Manufacturers also use it to make kitchenware and cutlery, including automotive exhaust systems. Just like carbon steel, it is easily available in the market.

Advantages

- Resistant to oxidation and corrosion
- Has a high ductility
- Ability to tolerate elevated temperatures
- Has a high strength to weight ratio

Disadvantages

- Has a thermal conductivity that is lower than carbon steel
- Has a high cost of both production and finishing
- Stronger grades such as duplex are difficult to forge
- Quite difficult to weld and handle

#: *Tool steel*

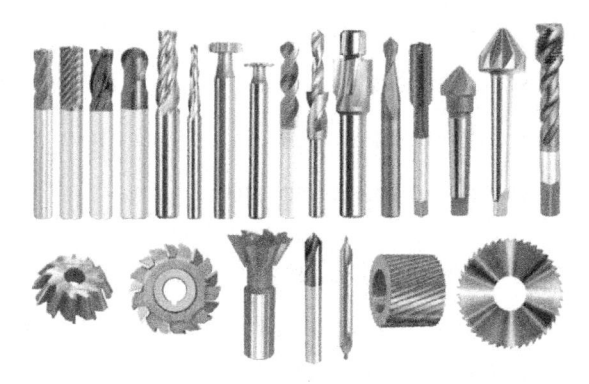

Tool steel

Tool steel makes cutting tools and other metal products. This steel is tough, wear-and-heat resistant because of its demanding applications, and composed of carbon and alloy steels. Manufacturers often improve tool steels' durability by adding alloying elements such as tungsten, cobalt, vanadium, and molybdenum.

Different tool steels composition

There are six distinctive classes of tool steels:

1: Water hardening tool steel

This tool steel is basic. It quickly hardens when introduced to water, making it prone to cracking and warping. Its resistance to high heat is low and easily softens at temperatures above 300 degrees Fahrenheit.

It is relatively cheap compared to alternative types of steel and mostly found at retailers selling metal or warehouses that supply steel. Its primary use is embossing taps and manufacturing cutlery and hand-operated cutting tools.

2: Cold work tool steel

This steel was developed in the 1860s by a metallurgist called Robert Mushet, who wanted to create steel that did not require water to harden. It hardens easily by air and quenching in oil; both ways reduce the risk of cracking.

Manufacturers improve this steel's hardness by adding small amounts of chromium, manganese, tungsten, or molybdenum, improving its tolerance to high temperature, increasing its hardness, and resistance to wear.

Its conventional forging temperatures range from 1575 degrees Fahrenheit to 2000 degrees Fahrenheit. Its primary use is to make machine parts bushings and camshafts. For a blacksmith hobbyist, it's most common use is woodworking tools and blades.

3: Shock Resisting tool steel

Like many other tool steel types, this steel contains considerable amounts of manganese, chromium, and molybdenum, increasing its hardness and strength. However, it's slightly different from the rest because of the addition of silicon, giving the material high resistance to deformation due to impact forces. They have a profound resistance to wear, making them the best candidate for making punches, chisels, and springs.

The best temperature to forge this steel is between 1800 degrees Fahrenheit and 2000 degrees Fahrenheit. After forging, blacksmiths must allow the steel to cool slowly and uniformly to minimize the stress. For this particular reason, an item formed from this steel cools in the furnace.

4: High-Speed tool steel

This type of steel originated from Robert Mushet's earlier development of the work tool steel.

At the turn of the 20th century, metallurgists from Bethlehem Steel experimented on the existing high-quality steel types and subjected them to extremely high temperatures than was generally done.

The final result was steel that withstood very high temperatures, later named high-speed tool steel. This steel has molybdenum and tungsten, which, when combined, form a 10% component of the total steel.

High-Speed tool steel's primary use is to make cutting tools such as gear cutters, drills and saw blades because it can withstand heat formed by friction. This characteristic further allows the tool to tolerate cutting at very high speeds, which is how this steel gets its name. This steel also finds use in manufacturing high—quality hand tools and woodturning tools.

Forging items from high-speed tool steel happens in temperatures between 1900 degrees Fahrenheit and 2050 degrees Fahrenheit. As is the case with shock-resistant tool steel, blacksmiths should hit this steel to this range uniformly and slowly. Gradual cooling items made from this steel after forging is also a requirement.

5: Hot work tool steel

This type of steel makes tools used at very high temperatures. Their primary use is in industries like pressure die casting, including applications like forging metal and glasswork. Its carbon content is low, up to 0.6%, but otherwise, it has high chromium, molybdenum, and tungsten content at a range of 6% to 25%.

However, some Hot work tool steel grades crack when subjected to water and high temperatures, especially those with high tungsten content. In general, however, most of these steel grades have excellent resistance to high temperature, deformation, shock, and wear. This particular steel gets forged in temperatures between 1700 degrees Fahrenheit and 2100 degrees Fahrenheit.

6: Special-purpose tool steels

These have a much higher alloy content, increasing its harden-ability and resistance to wear compared to water hardening tool steel.

From the above types of tool steels, you can see that you have a wide range of blacksmithing metals from which to choose.

Thus as a beginner, you need to select the correct type of tool steel for your specific application. When buying your steel, consider factors such as cost, resistance, hardness, and temperature.

#: *Scrap steel*

Steel is an exceptional product because it's easy to recycle—it's the world's highest recycled material. Steel does not deteriorate during the recycling process, and steel recycling emits less than 80% carbon dioxide than manufacturing new steel.

The steel recycling process starts with separating and sorting it from other metals. Then comes compacting and later shredding into small, easier-to-process pieces. These steel pieces then undergo the smelting process to become liquid steel. After that, the liquid steel gets refined using a suitable purification method. After the refining process, the liquid steel goes into a chamber where it cools into a solid.

Recycled steel can manufacture beams and pipes for various structural and industrial applications.

Advantages

- Lower carbon emissions
- Energy efficient
- Low cost
- Highly sustainable
- The recycling process does not compromise the physical properties

Disadvantages

- Producing high-quality steel depends on the sorting process
- The sorting requires extra caution

- It is challenging to control the alloying components in recycled steel

#: Fuel

No matter which type of forge you have, you will need fuel to produce heat. The fuel cost depends on the type of fuel you are going to use and the quantity required. The fuel most commonly used is coal.

Here is a description of some fuels used in blacksmith forging:

1: Lump Coal

As mentioned, coal is the most commonly used forging fuel. It gets smoky at first when lighted but clears away as the temperature increases. Bituminous coal is the most common coal; it's also inexpensive. Anthracite is the best coal to use. Lighting coal is difficult, but once it lights up, it burns hotter and longer.

Black Anthracite coal

2: Charcoal

Charcoal is the last fuel you should think of using because although it's readily available, on most occasions, it does not reach the temperature required to soften steel and iron without air flowing constantly. It is possible to burn a lot of charcoal without even achieving the required temperatures. If you are new to blacksmithing, you may try to use charcoal and see if it works on the projects you have in mind.

Restaurant Lumpwood charcoal

3: Propane

Propane is the best alternative to charcoal. It is a clean fuel that burns much hotter than charcoal and coal and has the advantage of being portable.

As a beginner blacksmith, propane would be the best fuel to use. Hence, building or buying a propane forge is the best choice. Using a forge will help you heat metal more completely and efficiently than an open torch.

Propane forges do not smoke like charcoal or coal forges but may produce a whooshing sound.

Calor propane tank

4: Electricity

You may decide to build an electric forge, which is OK, but remember that this type of forge involves electrical voltage, which can be highly dangerous. Risks include an electric shock, fire, and even death should you fail to follow safety precautions keenly.

If you are new to blacksmithing, electricity is not an ideal fuel source. Even as you gain experience, please do not attempt to use it unless you are 100% sure that you can safely work with mains voltage.

Best blacksmithing fuel choice for beginners

Now that you know four fuel options, which one should you choose? Well:

Charcoal is dirty and does not produce enough heat for forging successfully.

Coal burns longer and produces enough heat for forging. However, you have to ensure you have an efficient supplier who can provide a steady coal supply. Coal is also quite expensive.

Propane is readily available in the market and produces enough heat for forging. It's also a much cleaner fuel than charcoal and coal.

Propane is the best choice for your blacksmithing needs.

Because blacksmithing involves hot fire, you need to exercise a high degree of caution and safety when creating knives and other tools:

Chapter 4: Safety Rules Every Blacksmith Should Follow

Now that you know and understand the starter blacksmithing tools you need and planning your workshop, it is equally important to know the safety procedures you need to put in place.

From the knowledge you have gained so far, it quite clear that there is danger lurking everywhere inside a blacksmith's workshop because you will be dealing with toxic fumes, flames, flying scrapes, coal dust, and red-hot metal as you work. Given this, you can harm yourself or damage your property if you do not put in place proper safety procedures.

The first safety measure is reading all the safety manuals for the equipment you will use for blacksmithing. Burns are the most significant concerns; they can be mild or severe. Burns can occur on the skin, just as hot sparks can damage the eyes while hammering.

A fire outbreak is another possibility as blacksmiths work with fire most of the time. Fossil fuels like coal and charcoal can be dangerous to work with if you inhale the poisonous carbon monoxide released as these fuel types burn—they can be dangerous to the point of causing death. Hitting yourself with a hammer is another safety concern.

Don't forget that the repeated loud noises produced from the various blacksmith processes can also damage your ears. These noises will mostly come from hammering, grinding, and high-powered machines.

Understanding that many hazards can occur from blacksmithing, it is vital to learn about which safety measures to put in place.

Here are the safety measures you can put in place and follow. They could save your life or that of a friend.

: *Handle all materials in the workshop with care*

As a new blacksmith, do not assume that dark metal is cold metal. While in the workshop, treat every metal like it is very hot.

Some metal like steel will not glow red and can be hot enough to harm you. Therefore, wear heat-resistant gloves when forging metals in your workshop.

#: Wear protective accessories or gear when at your workshop

Do not wear any loose-fitting clothing that could get caught by your working tools. Remove any jewelry, including your wedding band. Secure your hair in place. Some of the protective gear and accessories you need the most include the following:

Apron

Aprons help protect the front part of your body, from your chest to the knee. Use a good leather apron. An apron also protects your clothes from dirt and will stick to your apron instead. Avoid wearing synthetic clothes; instead, wear clothes made from wool and cotton.

Apron

Protective eyewear

Safety glasses are one of the primary safety accessories you need; they protect you from flying chipping metals and hot sparks. Protect your eyes by wearing appropriate eyeglasses. Some are transparent, and others are dark-shaded; no matter which you prefer, get a pair that protects your eyes from UV rays.

Gateway Safety 36U50 Welding Safety Glasses

Gloves

You cannot underestimate the value of gloves. As a blacksmith, you will touch many hot objects, and hence, there is a risk of burning your palms. Your fingers are also at risk and need protection. Do not risk picking up the hot steel you are forging with your bare hands: use safety gloves

Blacksmith gloves

Respirator

When grinding, cutting, or sanding, you MUST protect your lungs because dust is harmful to your lungs. Over time, exposing yourself to blacksmithing dusk can cause irreversible damage to your respiratory system. You could wear a face mask, but a suitable respirator is a better recommendation.

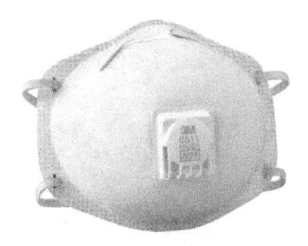

3M Particulate Respirator N95 8511 provides at least 95% filtration against various non-oil-based particles

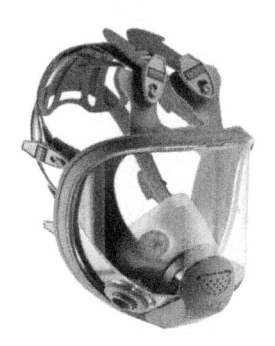

3M Ultimate FX Full Face-piece Respirator is excellent for knife-makers with facial hair

Safety Boots

You need to wear safety boots when you are in your workshop to protect your feet and legs. Hot objects could accidentally fall onto your feet, burning you badly. Safety boots can also protect you if you accidentally step on hot metals or sharp objects.

Men's Forge Steel Toe Waterproof Rubber Work Rain Boots

Earplugs

Many blacksmiths overlook the risk of ear damage due to noise, mainly because ear damage does not happen suddenly. It happens over time, sometimes taking months or even years before something noticeably wrong with your ears becomes apparent. You should take this type of slow injury seriously because it can be lethal.

Ear protection

#: Use an appropriate hammering technique

Repetitively swinging your hammer can harm your skeletal frame. As a beginner blacksmith, ensure that you use the proper form and technique to hammer your metal piece to avoid injury. Maintaining a particular posture for long can hinder the operations of your skeletal system.

#: Have proper ventilation in your workshop

As with any other workshop, proper ventilation is crucial in a blacksmithing workshop, and no matter which fuel you will be working with, you will require enough fresh air in your workshop.

You would not want to see people collapsing or fainting because they have either inhaled poisonous fumes, especially from coal or charcoal, or simply because there isn't enough air, do you? These fumes can also damage your respiratory system.

#: Perfect boy condition

Ensure you are in the proper frame of mind and that your body is in good condition when working in your workshop. Do not work if you are sick, drunk, tired, hungry, or feeling dizzy. Take breaks in between your work; this way, you will ensure you are alert and in good condition to work as a blacksmith.

#: First aid kit

Even when you work carefully as a blacksmith, you cannot 100% avoid minor injuries such as cuts, burns, scratches, etc. Thus, you should have a first aid kit complete with cut and burn remedies.

Make sure your first aid kit also has other items like bandages, cotton wool, methylated spirit, and anything else you feel you need. These will be your first response in case of an injury. If the injury is serious, a visit to the Emergency room should follow immediately.

Other than the safety measures mentioned above, there are many different measures you need to observe. They include—but are not limited to:

- Do not use damaged or malfunctioning tools such as anvils and hammers because, besides exposing you to hazards, it will also lower your productivity.

- Use the correct tool. For example, use the right tongs when lifting hot and heavy objects from the forge.

- When closing your workshop, never leave any fire burning in your forge. Put it out totally before leaving, irrespective of the type of forge you have.

- Learn as much as you can about your tools and machines of choice before using them. Before using any tool, read and understand the manufacturer's manual.

- Always check and ensure that the hammer's head affixes properly to its handle, which helps ensure it does not fly off, harming you or others or damaging anything.

- Work in a clean and tidy workshop. Avoid having clutter all over the place. Clear your floor of all debris and any sharp objects

- Be careful with any revolving parts.

- Return tools to their rightful place or position when done working with them.

- Ensure your electrical appliances are in good working condition and always appropriately connected.

- Orientate and monitor any visitor you may have in your workshop to ensure their safety.

It's impossible to give you comprehensive safety guidelines because every blacksmithing project is different. Generally, the main thing you need to do is do what you need to do to ensure your safety when working in the workshop at all times.

Chapter 5: Beginners Guide To Forging A Basic Knife

You have learned about the tools that you need to start your blacksmithing journey, now know how to create a workshop, and the safety rules to put in place to prevent injuries and damages.

That means you're ready to start forging:

Forging A Six-Inch Survival Knife

You can now embark on your very first project, which is forging a basic knife—a six-inch survival knife.

Let's begin:

Materials required

You will need the right material to make a knife that will function well without fail. You need to use the correct type of steel, sharpenable to a fine edge without fracturing or dulling.

Since you cannot use all metals to make knives, the best type of steel to use is:

- Tool steel

- carbon steel

- stainless steel

The thickness of the steel should be 1/16" (4/64" or 1.58mm) to make a kitchen or chef knife.

Equipment needed to make your knife

Making this knife requires basic equipment.

You will need a forge. A gas-powered forge is the best for beginners because it is easier to operate, clean, and cheaper than other forges. As mentioned earlier, Hell's Forge propane burner that costs $200 is the most ideal for beginners. You will also need an anvil, some tongs, a hammer, some grinder discs, sandpaper, a set of files, and a few odds and ends.

Create your design

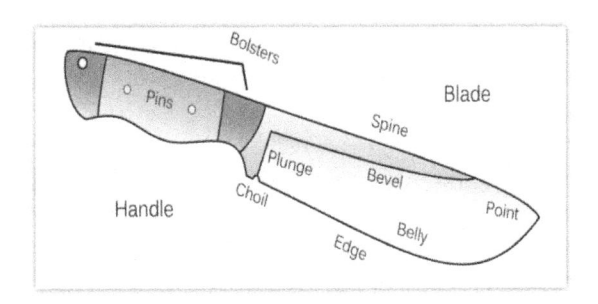

The next step is to come up with your knife's design. Start with outlining the dimensions of the knife you wish to make. The knife you will be making is a 6-inch long blade that has a diameter of 2 inches. The basic outline remains the same whether you will want a smaller, thicker, or longer.

A general blacksmith rule is that 2/3 of your survival knife will be the blade, while 1/3 will be your handle. For a 6-inch blade, always have an extra 3 inches for your handle. Whenever you come up with a design, always follow this guideline.

You will outline your design on a sheet of paper. You will then place your outline on top of the steel and use a pen to mark the metal; this will act as a rough blueprint while you hammer at your steel.

Forging your knife

Blacksmith forging a knife

Before placing your metal on the forge, take safety precautions by wearing protective eyewear, gloves, and other protective gear.

Check the color of your metal while it is in the forge. You will notice it changing to yellow when the temperature is between 2100 degrees Fahrenheit to 2200 degrees Fahrenheit. At this point, get your tongs and remove your metal piece from the flames: it has reached the required temperature.

You will then start hammering on the sides of your piece of metal, which will cause the metal to become thicker around the edges while the center remains the same. Afterward, lay your metal flat on the anvil and begin flattening it out by hammering.

Continue striking your metal, but this time, a little to the left instead of directly above the anvil's horn. The metal will slowly start bending to take the shape you want to curve. Use the anvil's flat side to hammer the metal flat and the horn to achieve the curves you want.

When you notice that your metal is folding over itself as you hammer, place the blade on the anvil and beat the edges back down until they are flat. An important aspect to note is that you should not spend too much time on the blade's tip, especially if it is curved or very thin. Work on it during your final forging session.

Switch to a smaller hammer as you finish working on your knife. A smaller hammer will give you better control and precision as you work on your knife, more so if you want to ensure that the bevel comes out well. You can remove any excess metal by placing it at the anvil's hardy-hole and hot cutting with a tool.

Drop Choil

Make sure you carve out the drop choil when you start forging your knife. You can do this before you begin curving, which we call half-face hammering, something done by placing your knife half-way off the anvil.

Beveling the blade

As you get close to the shape you want, start beveling the blade by hammering both sides of the blade to thin out the edge you will sharpen. Hammer it at an angle to achieve this.

As you apply blows onto your blade, the steel will be pushing up toward the spine. At this point, ensure you form a nice wedge shape that joins the blade's cutting edge.

Annealing the knife

Annealing is the process of softening your knife so you can continue working on it with hand tools, grinders, sandpaper, files, and other tools.

Heat the knife until it turns red-orange. Check if it sticks to a magnet. If it does not, start to cool it down slowly, which can do by submerging it fully in some sand. Allow it to cool down, and then finish working on it later before fixing the handle.

Putting a handle on your knife

The handle has two different parts: the bolster, the darker wood, and the handle, the lighter wood. Therefore, the handle has four pieces, two on each side. You will glue these four pieces in place and pin them with brass. The brass rods in the handle are 1/8 inch, while the bolster is 1/16 inch, as shown below.

Use the knife as a template to drill holes into the four pieces of wood cut roughly to the approximate size of the bolster and handle. Using wooden dowels, attach the pieces to the knife temporarily.

With a rasp, belt sander, get your desired shape and size and obtain a nice finish using sandpaper. Once you achieve the correct shape with a good finish, remove the bolster handle pieces, and set them aside.

Hardening and Tempering your blade

Heat your forge and place your knife in.

Get another piece of long metal, place it in the forge, and heat it. Then get a bucket and put oil in it; any oil will work. You can use vegetable oil, motor oil, even transmission fluid. Remove your long metal and dip it into the bucket of oil.

That will bring up the temperature of the oil, which makes for a better tempering and hardening. Heat your knife to red-orange, paying attention to the blade and point. Test if the magnet sticks to it. If it does, submerge it totally in the oil and swirl it around.

When you remove it from the oil, you can now finish off the blade. Grind it using Emory paper, which gives your blade a great and smooth look. After using the Emory paper, you can buff it using a buffing wheel. Be very cautious when using a buffing wheel; it can grab your knife and fling it at you.

Once your knife has cooled, test how hard it is with a file. Run your file lightly over it; you should hear a glassy sound. The file should also run over your knife without grabbing at anything.

Clean your blade on both sides with sandpaper or Emory paper, making sure to get it very clean. You are now ready to temper your knife. Slowly raise the blade's temperature. The temperature along the spine should be higher than that of the cutting edge, which can achieve by watching out for color changes. The spine should get to a plum color, and the cutting edge will have a wheat color.

As you can see from the image above, you should place the spine closer to the fire, with the cutting edge further away from the fire. The spine will heat up first and slowly transmit the heat to the blade's cutting.

As soon as the blade's spine gets a plum color and the cutting edge to wheat, dip it into the oil and lock it in. Clean the knife with an Emory paper. The next step is to mount the handle onto the knife.

Fixing the handle onto the knife

Sandpaper the inner parts of the handle pieces, the edges you will glue to your knife. Use a hacksaw to cut your pins from a brass rod. Cut two 1/16 inch pins and two 1/8 inch pins. Use the wooden pins to guide how long you will cut your brass pins, but make sure they are slightly longer because you will file these pins once you install them into the handle.

Test your pins to check if they fit into your knife and handle holes. You don't want to struggle to fix them when everything has wet glue on it.

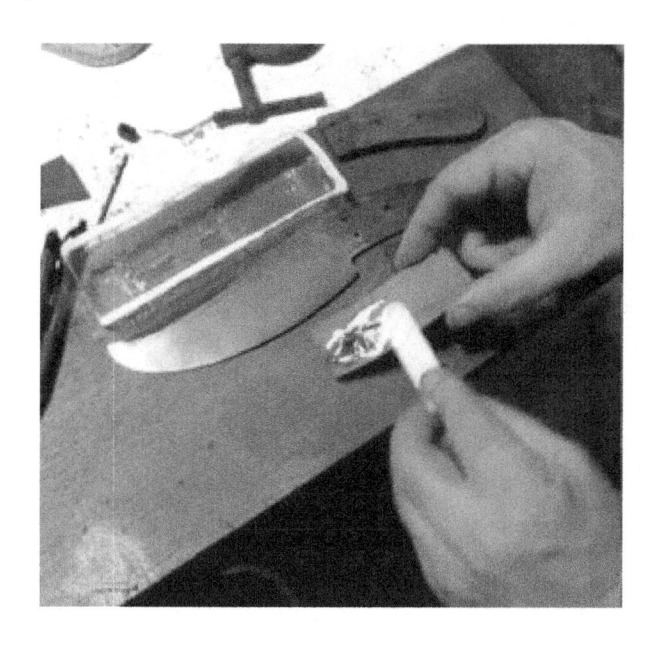

Go ahead and mix two parts of epoxy glue, such as the five-minute Gorilla glue. However, you can use the twenty-minute epoxy glue, giving you more time to fix your knife correctly.

Apply the glue on the four pieces of the handle. Affix your pieces to the knife and insert the pins, then use a small hammer to tap the pins in. Clamp your knife and wait for it to dry for 90 minutes before handling it and 24 hours for a complete cure. Avoid clamping on the pins.

After the glue has set, you can clean it up with acetone. Use a file to fine the brass pins down. File the handle to have a good finish and polish it—you can apply a few Tung oil coats.

Sharpen your blade, and your knife is ready for use.

Chapter 6: The Best Projects For A Beginner Blacksmith

There are many simple projects that a beginner blacksmith can tackle, many of which are good practice before embarking on more challenging projects. You can even make the items and sell them to buy more tools to make larger, more complex items.

Other than a knife, here are some beginner-friendly blacksmithing projects:

Simple J Hook

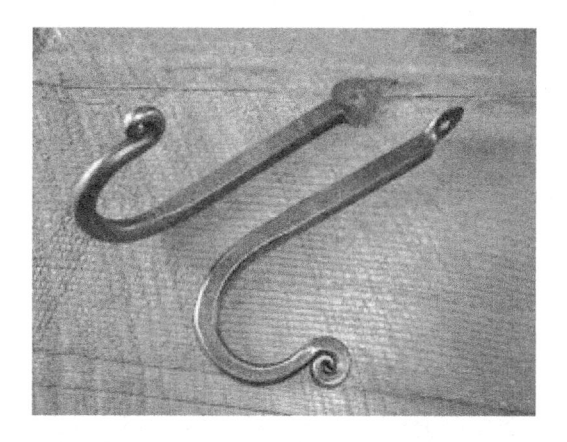

J hooks are one of the simplest items you can make as a blacksmith. You can also use them to hang various items in your home or office.

To make a J hook, you will need a pair of tongs, a chisel, a hammer, an anvil, a forge, and a 3/8 steel bar.

Heat one of the rod by placing it in the forge, then once hot, create a point with your hammer. To make the point, beat the end of the rod while rotating it. Extend the taper of the point by 1½-inches.

Once your rod has obtained a tapered end, heat it again and smooth out the edges by striking and rotating it frequently. You will get a more rounded design, with any defined edges removed. After designing your taper the way you wanted it, reheat your rod and create a U shape. Bend the tapered point in on itself to form a curled end.

Hot cut your rod into your desired length. After cutting the hook, straighten it out as required and hammer the straight end flat to create a mounting spot.

Punch

All blacksmiths need a punch at one time or another because it helps creates holes in your projects when needed. You can use any size of rod depending on why you need it. Any metal rod will work for this project.

The tools you will need are a hammer, tongs, an anvil, and a small forge.

Heat your rod and cut it to the desired length. Taper the end into a point with your hammer. The end of your point should be flat. Round off the taper's edges by striking and rotating it repeatedly.

Finish your punch by grinding it and then polishing it. You may also choose to leave it unfinished for a rougher look.

Fire Poker

A fire poker is a simple blacksmith beginner project you can give as a gift, sell, or use in your home to tend to your fireplaces.

To make your fire poker, you will require a long metal bar, a vice, tongs, an anvil, and a forge.

Begin by tapering one end of the metal bar, then make a loop on the tapered end by curling it around itself. To acquire a smooth coil, reheat, and shape to make it smooth. While the rod is in the vice, continue to twist this end of the taper around the rod. On the opposite end, you will create a tapered point that is shorter.

Bottle Opener

This project is simple and ideal for a new blacksmith. You can make one to sell, to give as a gift, or for your use. You will require a punch, a hammer, an anvil, and a forge for this project. You can use any metal bar for this project.

Heat and flatten one end of the bar. Punch and shape a large hole in it, then finish by creating a lip to catch and pull open bottle tops.

Decorative Heart

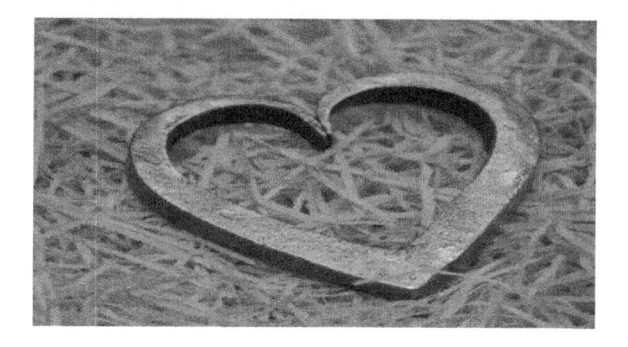

A decorative heart is a wonderful gift to make for a loved one or to sell. To make a heart, you need a hammer, tongs, an anvil, a forge, and a ½ inch square bar.

Using the anvil, create the curved shape of a heart from your rod. With your hammer, taper the ends of the bar to create the shape of a heart. Curl both ends inwards towards each other until they meet in the middle to create a heart shape.

The shape of the heart will vary depending on your likes.

Leaf Key Chain

A leaf-shaped key chain is a good challenge for a beginner blacksmith. This project is a little more involving than other much simpler ones. For a successful project, you need a metal bar, a hammer, an anvil, and a forge.

Taper the pointed end, then, using your hammer, beat the end of the bar flat to form the shape of a leaf. Curl the stem to form a closed loop.

Rounding Hammer

A hammer is another great project that will challenge beginners. To forge a hammer as a beginner, you will need to manage your metal, heat it properly, and skillfully shape it into your desired hammer.

Use a 3-inch long billet of 2-inch round 1045 steel. Heat your steel and then hammer it into the general shape you want your hammer to have. Once your metal has a square shape with beveled edges, begin punching the hole where you will fix the handle. Rotate your hammer after every few blows.

Anatomy of the Hammer

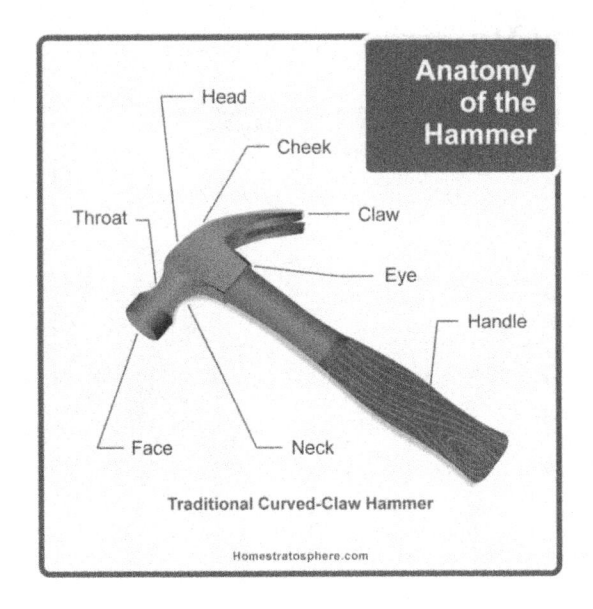

Traditional Curved-Claw Hammer

Homestratosphere.com

After completing the eye of your hammer, it's time to shape the cheeks. Since you do not want to deform the just-created eye, use the drift itself to hammer and bolster the eye as you hammer the middle part into the thickness, shape, and texture you want your hammer to have in the end.

After completing the cheeks, create the throat, and develop any face combination you want. If you want a simple rounding hammer, put a face on both sides, which you will dress later to form a roundness of a different degree.

Towards the end of the process, you don't need to do much forging. Applying heat treatment to a rounding hammer is critical because this tool will make endless blows against the anvil and hot metal. Therefore, the hammer needs to get back to a specific temperature, allowed to cool down slowly to room temperature, which is better than quenching or annealing the metal. The best time to mark it is when it is very hot. After the hammer has cooled down, you can fix the handle.

Dinner Bell

A dinner bell is one of the easiest items a new blacksmith can make, with the triangular dinner bell being a good place to start. Take a small thin piece of metal. Heat it and bend it into a triangle. Take another thin piece of metal and forge out a small clinger.

Tongs

To make your tongs, you will need a thin metal piece, a hammer, a forge, channel locks or vice grips, an anvil, a rod for bolting, and an ax head or chisel.

Measure and mark the length of the metal you want to use. Leave some wiggle room because the process of drawing out the metal elongates it. Heat the part you need to cut out, then flatten your metal along the seams, which will guide you to where the edge will be. Start to flatten it on one end and then work down the metal by heating it and hitting it on the anvil.

Heat the end part you want to be your bit. Using your vice grips, twist the metal at 90 degrees. For the second piece of metal, twist it in the opposite direction. If you do not do this, you will end up with two identical metal pieces.

Now create the arc for the jaws, making sure that they form an eclipse when you assemble the two metal pieces. You do this by placing your metal, making sure the flat end is placed parallel to the anvil. The handle should be perpendicular to the anvil. Heat this section inside the forge and then proceed to round it off.

Flip your metal at 180 degrees from its last position to ensure the part with the twisted bit bent down is facing upwards. Heat the straight part of the handle directly below the jaw's curved part and bang it down. Hit it until placed flat down on the anvil; it will be on the same line as the handle. Both pieces should be a mirror of each other.

Place the two metal bars on top of each other to appear as it would when completed. Then mark the center where they intersect. Heat it and punch a hole in it, ensuring the hole you create is the same diameter as the rod you have for the bolt to have a friction fit. Punch a hole in both metal pieces.

Test and check that the bolt you will use fits in both pieces. Place the entire tong in the forge where the bolt is and heat it. When it's hot, go ahead and peen out the bolt. Flatten both ends to set the two pieces of metal together permanently.

Don't start opening and closing the tongs until it cools off completely; otherwise, you will go back a few steps and start again.

You now have your new tongs.

Loggerhead

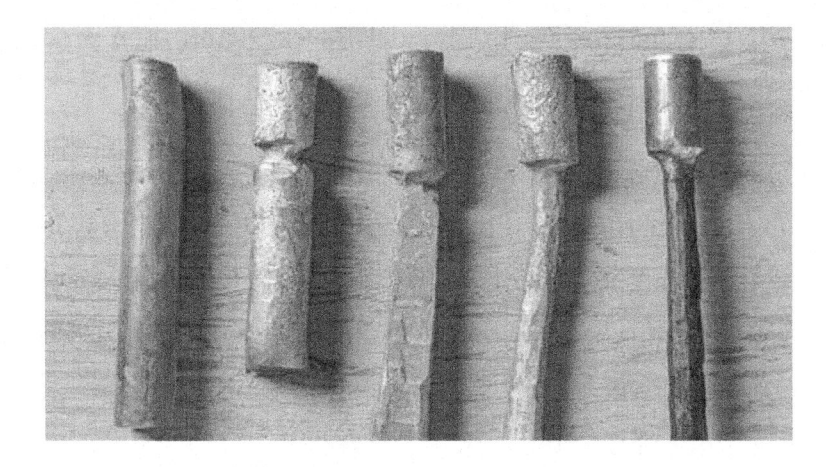

Loggerhead is a tool used in the olden days to heat drinks. It works like a modern microwave using the quenching method, where you place a hot piece of metal in your drink to heat it. To make this item, you will need a 4 inch round bar.

From one end of the bar, forge out the neck between 2 and 3 inches in length. Cut off the excess stock and leave enough metal length to forge your favorite handle. Finally, wire brushes well and apply a food-safe finish.

A typical logger-head heating up a drink

Loop Opener

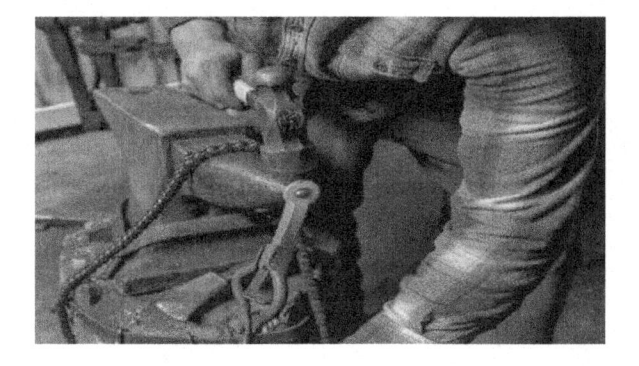

Heat a piece of metal and flatten the first 1-inch using half-face blows. Also, ensure to orient the lip that you see sticking out of the spike's head, ensuring the shoulder created on the tip is on the opposite side of the opener. Doing this will make the final product more ergonomic.

Use a slot punch to create an approximately 5/8" hole at the center of the tip, then use the horn to enlarge the loop to 1" and 1¼" in diameter. Keep shifting the loop with each blow to even it out uniformly. Make sure you also flip the metal piece after several hits to avoid beveling the hole in one direction only.

As the loop gets heated evenly, hit it rearwards to the spike to form the opener's oval shape. If it does not form symmetrically, you can open it again on the horn and re-create it. Finish by forging the tab that will catch the bottle cap using a ball punch.

Herb Chopper

As the name suggests, a herb chopper is a kitchen tool used to cut herbs; it can be one or two-handed. When forging, take extra caution to taper both handles so that they match. Stainless steel is an excellent material for this kitchen tool as it will not rust.

Starting with a 16" flat stock, offset one end at 2" using the half-face blows technique. Forge a taper that is approximately 5 ½". On the remaining stock, forge a bevel at the edge to create the blade.

Work on both sides of the blade and take caution to forge the blade down the metal piece evenly, working back and forth frequently instead of heavily at each spot. Doing this will give you a symmetrical blade and curve to the chopper from the spread metal.

Curl the tip and then create the handle in the same direction as the blade. Create a bigger curve at the back onto the top of the chopper. You may have to mark the bends to refer back to each handle and work on each side freehand.

Finally, use a file or grinder to sharpen the blade to your desired sharpness and also fix any asymmetry on the blade. Wire brush and apply a food-safe finish. Oil slightly to stop rust.

Egg Spoon and Ladle

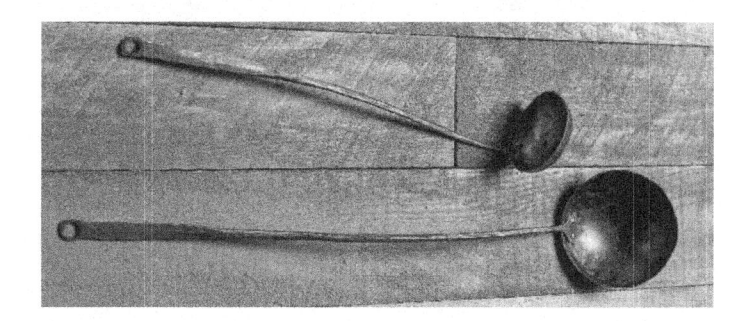

You will need a 16 gauge sheet metal or 6" x 6", 8-inch round stock run long, or 10-gauge copper wire. For the egg spoon, draw out a 6-inch circle in the metal sheet and cut it out using a cold-cutting grinder or chisel. For the ladle, make a 4" to 5" circle. Use a file or grinder to clean up the edges.

Dish the piece with a rounded hammer or a ball peen. Make the bowl for the ladle deeper than that of the egg spoon. Make the loop at a 90-degree angle from the round bar and cut off a 2-inch section from the excess. Ensure you flatten this section slightly and clamp it in the vise.

Isolate ¾ inch of the end of the bar using a fullering tool and then round it off. Taper the neck back 3 inches. With a cross-peen hammer, hit the ends to form an oval shape whose wide wide section is perpendicular to the handle's shaft. Go ahead and curve the oval end to fit the curve of the bowl.

For the egg spoon, gradually forge a 16-inch taper towards the spread end. For the ladle, forge an 11-inch taper. Leave out some metal at the tip to support the bowl end. Flatten out 6 inches beyond the taper and cut off at that particular point. With a slot punch and ½ inch drift, create a hole at the top of the handle. Clean the hole using the horn. Bevel the handle's edges, creating a look that resembles a compressed pyramid.

To assemble and finish the bowl and ladle, drill out two holes a little bigger than a 10-gauge wire in the bowl and handle. Use the 10-gauge copper for the rivets. For the egg spoon, curve the handle to make it level with the bowl when you hold the handle at approximately 30 degrees. For the ladle, curve the handle to ensure the bowl is level with the handle when held approximately 80 degrees.

Colonial Spatula

The traditional spatula is a wonderful way to practice your hammering techniques. You will need 4" x 1" steel. Forge a shoulder 13/4 inch from one end. Hammer half-face blows on the near side of the anvil and forge a swell. Neck in ¾" from the first shoulder on the ¼" face.

With a cross-pein hammer, forge a trough down the center of the blade, gradually widening symmetrically. Leave the edges thicker until you finish spreading the metal. As you hold the spatula in line with the horn of the anvil, hammer out the peen marks.

Draw out the remainder of the handle 31/6" x ½." Neck in the handle 1" from the blade. Turn 90 degrees so that the blade is upright and shoulder with a half-face blow. Move up 11/4" and apply half-face blow near the edge of the anvil. Create an octagon, then round off the isolated area to create a decorative "barrel."

Use the cross-peen hammer to spread the shoulder on each side of the barrel. Ensuring it is at 45 degrees, create a cusp which increases the strength of the transition points.

Use half-face blows; offset ¾" from the top of the handle, which is the hook. From the back of the handle from the barrel, make a fuller shallow. Forge the offset part to a point and create a small curl towards the offset. Afterward, quench the curl and close the loop with the horn of the anvil. Heat the offset between 20 and 30 degrees before curling it to form a rounded loop.

You can correct any misalignment at this stage. Grind or trim excess metal from the spatula blade and then proceed to cold hammer the edges of the spatula. Use a file to refine it.

Meat Skewer

You will need a long thin metal bar to make your meat skewer. You will also need a forge, an anvil, a hammer, and a vice.

Place one end of the bar in the forge and heat it. Curl the end in on itself to achieve a decorative end. Continue to form a larger loop to complete the skewer's handle. By placing the skewer in a vice, turn it to make an even twist along the bar.

Heart Decorative Bowl

A heart bowl is a great gift for anniversaries, weddings, valentine's day, and other events. To make such a bowl, you will need a metal sheet, a swage block, a hammer, and an anvil.

After you forge a heart-shaped metal, move it to a swage block then proceed to hammer to make a rounded bowl shape. You can either finish it off by letting it have a rough look or polish it. You can make these bowls into any size you wish; you can also stamp names or dates to personalize for each customer.

Drawer Pulls

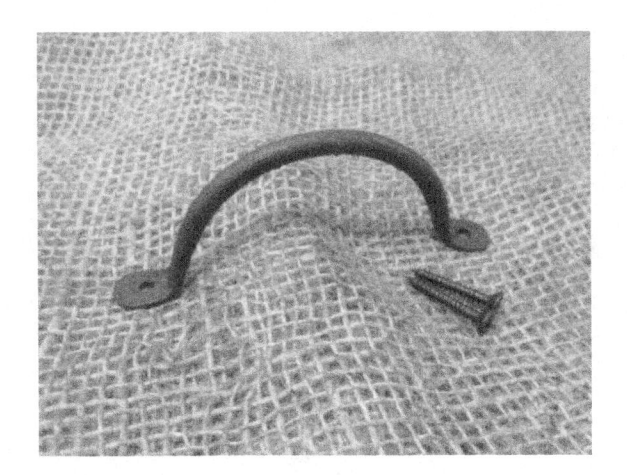

The drawer pull is a super easy and quick to make tool. To make the drawer pull, you will need a drill press, a small length of metal stock, tongs, hammer, anvil, and a forge.

Heat the bar's ends and hammer them flat to form the drawer handle feet. Bend the feet so that they are at the correct angle for installation.

Heat the drawer pull's middle part and curve it around the anvil horn until it takes on an arched shape. There is no particular rule to creating the shape; you can shape it to your preferred style. Use a punch to drill the holes.

Conclusion

Blacksmithing is a wonderful hobby.

In this book, you have learned:

- The basics of the tools you need to start forging various tools; as you can imagine, there're other tools that you will learn about it as you continue with your new trade.

- We've learned how to create a functional blacksmithing workshop, which is crucial because you will be handling fire, and other harmful fuels, including equipment. You need to take a lot of care when in your workshop. Do not ignore the safety measures which could save your life and that of those who frequent your workshop.

- We looked at how to forge basic items, which are a great way to get started as a beginners blacksmith.

Since you now have all the knowledge you need, commit to gaining as much experience as possible, and gradually progress towards forging complex items. As your skills develop, don't be surprised if your trade starts making money: many people earn a decent living from forging different things.

Good luck on your journey, and thank you for reading this book:

PS: I'd like your feedback. If you are happy with this book, please leave a review on Amazon.

Please leave a review for this book on Amazon by visiting the page below:

https://amzn.to/2VMR5qr

Made in United States
North Haven, CT
03 December 2021